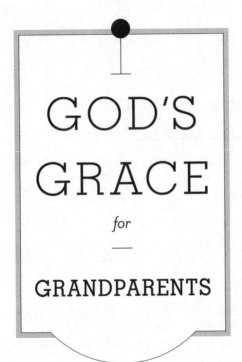

GOD'S GRACE

for

GRANDPARENTS

PUBLISHING GROUP

NASHVILLE, TENNESSEE

978-1-5359-1748-3

Published by B&H Publishing Group
Nashville, Tennessee

Dewey Decimal Classification: 234.1
Subject Heading: GRACE (THEOLOGY) / HOPE / SELF-CONFIDENCE

1 2 3 4 5 6 7 8 · 22 21 20 19 18

CONTENTS

INTRODUCTION

Life tends to maneuver us into categories, into penciled-in bubbles on the random identification form. Some of them we like; some we don't. Some we actively seek out and continue to pursue; some were sitting there waiting for us and won't turn us loose.

But one thing we all know: deep inside these simple boxes and check marks reside entire worlds crawling with complication, challenge, and difficulty. Even if easy to get into, they are rarely so easy to faithfully, successfully, and steadily keep going through.

As a grandparent, you may often feel inadequate to the task ahead of you. You may not have the energy you once had to chase children around the yard, or you may wish your grandchildren lived closer. You try maximizing the jobs your particular box (or boxes) entails, yet they maddeningly resist being colored all the way to the edges. You're closing one chapter and starting a whole new one.

The reason this book exists is because God's grace never met a check box it couldn't fill with hope, peace, direction, and perspective—with motivation, counsel, freedom, and opportunity. This book is here, and is now yours, because the Bible not only speaks timelessly to everyone but specifically to you . . . with grace. God's grace. Sufficient to every place. Even to the places you're living this very moment.

ANXIETY

Beneath the anxieties that torment us is a need to feel in control of our circumstances—but our peace is found in remembering that the Creator of the whole universe has us safely in the palm of His hand.

∽

"Therefore I tell you: Don't worry about your life, what you will eat or what you will drink; or about your body, what you will wear. Isn't life more than food and the body more than clothing? Consider the birds of the sky: They don't sow or reap or gather into barns, yet your heavenly Father feeds them. Aren't you worth more than they? Can any of you add one moment to his life-span by worrying?"
   Matthew 6:25–27

∽

"Peace I leave with you. My peace I give to you. I do not give to you as the world gives. Don't let your heart be troubled or fearful."
   John 14:27

Don't worry about anything, but in everything, through prayer and petition with thanksgiving, present your requests to God. And the peace of God, which surpasses all understanding, will guard your hearts and minds in Christ Jesus.
      Philippians 4:6–7

∽

For God has not given us a spirit of fear, but one of power, love, and sound judgment.
      2 Timothy 1:7

∽

Humble yourselves, therefore, under the mighty hand of God, so that he may exalt you at the proper time, casting all your cares on him, because he cares about you.
      1 Peter 5:6–7

∽

Heavenly Father, I entrust to You my health, my future, my kids, my grandkids, and all the things that feel outside of my control, knowing that Your peace will guard my heart and mind.

ASSURANCE OF FAITH

No matter when you came to faith, whether as a small child or very late in life, you are a coheir with Christ and sealed by His Holy Spirit.

❦

"Truly I tell you, anyone who hears my word and believes him who sent me has eternal life and will not come under judgment but has passed from death to life."
John 5:24

❦

You did not receive a spirit of slavery to fall back into fear. Instead, you received the Spirit of adoption, by whom we cry out, "Abba, Father!" The Spirit himself testifies together with our spirit that we are God's children, and if children, also heirs—heirs of God and coheirs with Christ—if indeed we suffer with him so that we may also be glorified with him.
Romans 8:15–17

If you confess with your mouth, "Jesus is Lord," and believe in your heart that God raised him from the dead, you will be saved. One believes with the heart, resulting in righteousness, and one confesses with the mouth, resulting in salvation.

Romans 10:9–10

∽

And since we have a great high priest over the house of God, let us draw near with a true heart in full assurance of faith, with our hearts sprinkled clean from an evil conscience and our bodies washed in pure water. Let us hold on to the confession of our hope without wavering, since he who promised is faithful.

Hebrews 10:21–23

∽

I have written these things to you who believe in the name of the Son of God so that you may know that you have eternal life.

1 John 5:13

∽

Thank You, Lord Jesus, that I can draw near to You, for You are faithful.

AUTHORITY

Throughout your life you have held positions of authority in many areas—in your family, profession, church, and community—but ultimately God is in control of every sphere of life.

∽

Then he said to them, "Give, then, to Caesar the things that are Caesar's, and to God the things that are God's." When they heard this, they were amazed. So they left him and went away.
  Matthew 22:21–22

∽

Jesus came near and said to them, "All authority has been given to me in heaven and on earth."
  Matthew 28:18

∽

Let everyone submit to the governing authorities, since there is no authority except from God, and the authorities that exist are instituted by God.
  Romans 13:1

For this reason God highly exalted him
and gave him the name
that is above every name,
so that at the name of Jesus
every knee will bow—
in heaven and on earth
and under the earth—
and every tongue will confess
that Jesus Christ is Lord,
to the glory of God the Father.
Philippians 2:9–11

❦

Submit to every human authority because of the Lord, whether to the
emperor as the supreme authority or to governors as those sent out
by him to punish those who do what is evil and to praise those who do
what is good. For it is God's will that you silence the ignorance of foolish
people by doing good.
1 Peter 2:13–15

❦

Lord God, I praise You for granting me wisdom and
grace to be a mirror of godly authority in my life, and
I willingly submit to Your authority in all things.

BEAUTY

All of creation is ablaze with the beauty of the Lord—look for it in the sunsets, the stars, the blooms of flowers in spring, the glow of a happy grandchild.

෯

I have asked one thing from the LORD;
it is what I desire:
to dwell in the house of the LORD
all the days of my life,
gazing on the beauty of the LORD
and seeking him in his temple.
   Psalm 27:4

෯

I will praise you
because I have been remarkably and wondrously made.
Your works are wondrous,
and I know this very well.
   Psalm 139:14

Charm is deceptive and beauty is fleeting,
but a woman who fears the LORD will be praised.
Proverbs 31:30

⌘

You are absolutely beautiful, my darling;
there is no imperfection in you.
Song of Solomon 4:7

⌘

Don't let your beauty consist of outward things like elaborate hairstyles
and wearing gold jewelry, but rather what is inside the heart—the
imperishable quality of a gentle and quiet spirit, which is of great worth
in God's sight.
1 Peter 3:3–4

⌘

Heavenly Father, I thank You and praise You for the
beauty You have poured out on this earth, which
heals and blesses the hearts that behold it.

BLESSINGS

The way to joy is to take notice of the abundance of blessings in our lives every day and to praise and thank the Lord for such grace.

⌘

"May the LORD bless you and protect you; may the LORD make his face shine on you and be gracious to you; may the LORD look with favor on you and give you peace."
> *Numbers 6:24–26*

⌘

Indeed, we have all received grace upon grace from his fullness, for the law was given through Moses; grace and truth came through Jesus Christ.
> *John 1:16–17*

And God is able to make every grace overflow to you, so that in every way, always having everything you need, you may excel in every good work.
    2 Corinthians 9:8

                   ∽

Blessed is the God and Father of our Lord Jesus Christ, who has blessed us with every spiritual blessing in the heavens in Christ.
    Ephesians 1:3

                   ∽

And my God will supply all your needs according to his riches in glory in Christ Jesus.
    Philippians 4:19

                   ∽

Heavenly Father, I thank You and praise You for all the ways You have shown me mercy and grace, and I ask for the blessing of Your presence throughout this day.

CARING

Grandparents play a special role in young people's lives: in many ways you reflect the nature of God as a shelter and refuge during life's stormy seasons.

∽

"I give you a new command: Love one another. Just as I have loved you, you are also to love one another. By this everyone will know that you are my disciples, if you love one another."
    John 13:34–35

∽

Carry one another's burdens; in this way you will fulfill the law of Christ.
    Galatians 6:2

Therefore, as we have opportunity, let us work for the good of all,
especially for those who belong to the household of faith.
        Galatians 6:10

✍

Everyone should look out not only for his own interests, but also for the
interests of others.
        Philippians 2:4

✍

> *Dear Jesus, grant me the opportunity*
> *to extend caring and compassion to someone*
> *who may need encouragement today.*

CHANGE

Getting older can be fraught with uncertainty and unease, but we can rest in the promise that Christ is eternal and unchanging.

∽

There is an occasion for everything, and a time for every activity under heaven.
>   *Ecclesiastes 3:1*

∽

"Do not remember the past events, pay no attention to things of old. Look, I am about to do something new; even now it is coming. Do you not see it? Indeed, I will make a way in the wilderness, rivers in the desert."
>   *Isaiah 43:18–19*

"Because I, the LORD, have not changed, you descendants of Jacob have not been destroyed."
  Malachi 3:6

∽

Therefore, if anyone is in Christ, he is a new creation; the old has passed away, and see, the new has come!
  2 Corinthians 5:17

∽

Jesus Christ is the same yesterday, today, and forever.
  Hebrews 13:8

∽

Lord Jesus, no matter what the future brings, may I take heart that You are with me until the end of the age.

CHILDREN

Among a grandparent's greatest joys is time spent with children and grandchildren, who are our heritage and legacy.

✍

Sons are indeed a heritage from the LORD,
offspring, a reward.
Like arrows in the hand of a warrior
are the sons born in one's youth.
Happy is the man who has filled his quiver with them.
They will never be put to shame
when they speak with their enemies at the city gate.
    Psalm 127:3–5

✍

Even a young man is known by his actions—
by whether his behavior is pure and upright.
    Proverbs 20:11

When Jesus saw it, he was indignant and said to them, "Let the little children come to me. Don't stop them, because the kingdom of God belongs to such as these."
Mark 10:14

༄

Fathers, don't stir up anger in your children, but bring them up in the training and instruction of the Lord.
Ephesians 6:4

༄

Children, obey your parents in everything, for this pleases the Lord.
Colossians 3:20

༄

Heavenly Father, please guard and protect my children and grandchildren with Your tender love and mercy.

COMFORT

None of us are immune from hardships, loss, and grief, but we can take heart that no matter what has happened, the Lord is quick to comfort us.

⁓

Even when I go through the darkest valley,
I fear no danger,
for you are with me;
your rod and your staff—they comfort me.
>   *Psalm 23:4*

⁓

Remember your word to your servant;
you have given me hope through it.
This is my comfort in my affliction:
Your promise has given me life.
>   *Psalm 119:49–50*

As a mother comforts her son, so I will comfort you, and you will be comforted in Jerusalem.
   Isaiah 66:13

~

"Blessed are those who mourn, for they will be comforted."
   Matthew 5:4

~

Blessed be the God and Father of our Lord Jesus Christ, the Father of mercies and the God of all comfort. He comforts us in all our affliction, so that we may be able to comfort those who are in any kind of affliction, through the comfort we ourselves receive from God.
   2 Corinthians 1:3–4

~

Dear God, thank You for comforting me and healing my heart in times of trial, and may I be a source of comfort for others.

COMPASSION

The Lord has commanded that we love our neighbors as ourselves and also love our enemies—we demonstrate compassion by acting out of love in the best interests of others.

❧

Yet he was compassionate;
he atoned for their iniquity
and did not destroy them.
He often turned his anger aside
and did not unleash all his wrath.
    Psalm 78:38

❧

When he went ashore, he saw a large crowd and had compassion on
them, because they were like sheep without a shepherd. Then he began
to teach them many things.
    Mark 6:34

Carry one another's burdens; in this way you will fulfill the law of Christ.
  Galatians 6:2

∽

*And be kind and compassionate to one another, forgiving one another,
just as God also forgave you in Christ.*
  Ephesians 4:32

∽

*Lord, may Your Holy Spirit fill my heart
and soul with concern for others so that
I may be a willing conduit of Your love.*

CONTENTMENT

The fastest way to contentment is through trust and thanksgiving—take note of the abundant goodness in your life, knowing God never fails to provide.

✍

"So don't worry, saying, 'What will we eat?' or 'What will we drink?' or 'What will we wear?' For the Gentiles eagerly seek all these things, and your heavenly Father knows that you need them. But seek first the kingdom of God and his righteousness, and all these things will be provided for you. Therefore don't worry about tomorrow, because tomorrow will worry about itself. Each day has enough trouble of its own."
    Matthew 6:31–34

✍

He then told them, "Watch out and be on guard against all greed, because one's life is not in the abundance of his possessions."
    Luke 12:15

I don't say this out of need, for I have learned to be content in whatever circumstances I find myself. I know both how to make do with little, and I know how to make do with a lot. In any and all circumstances I have learned the secret of being content—whether well fed or hungry, whether in abundance or in need.

Philippians 4:11–12

∽

But godliness with contentment is great gain. For we brought nothing into the world, and we can take nothing out. If we have food and clothing, we will be content with these.

1 Timothy 6:6–8

∽

Keep your life free from the love of money. Be satisfied with what you have, for he himself has said, I will never leave you or abandon you.

Hebrews 13:5

∽

*Lord, I praise You for Your faithfulness
in my life and ask that You help me to rest
contentedly in the life to which You have called me.*

DEPRESSION

When your heart is broken and your mind is burdened, hold fast to the truth that God is the God of all comfort, who comforts us in all our affliction so that we may be able to comfort others.

❧

The LORD sits enthroned over the flood;
the LORD sits enthroned, King forever.
The LORD gives his people strength;
the LORD blesses his people with peace.
    Psalm 29:10–11

❧

Answer me quickly, LORD; my spirit fails.
Don't hide your face from me,
or I will be like those
going down to the Pit.
Let me experience
your faithful love in the morning,
for I trust in you.
Reveal to me the way I should go
because I appeal to you.
    Psalm 143:7–8

Do not fear, for I am with you;
do not be afraid, for I am your God.
I will strengthen you; I will help you;
I will hold on to you with my righteous right hand.
       Isaiah 41:10

❧

The LORD is near the brokenhearted;
he saves those crushed in spirit.
       Psalm 34:18

❧

"I will give you the treasures of darkness
and riches from secret places,
so that you may know that I am the LORD.
I am the God of Israel, who calls you by your name."
       Isaiah 45:3

❧

Dear Jesus, You were a man of sorrows and
acquainted with grief—please fill my heart with
Your strength and bring me Your peace.

DISCERNMENT

The Holy Spirit is our ever-present Helper who grants us wisdom so that we can know and do the will of God.

⁓

So give your servant a receptive heart to judge your people and to discern between good and evil. For who is able to judge this great people of yours?
     1 Kings 3:9

⁓

And I pray this: that your love will keep on growing in knowledge and every kind of discernment, so that you may approve the things that are superior and may be pure and blameless in the day of Christ.
     Philippians 1:9–10

⁓

Don't stifle the Spirit. Don't despise prophecies, but test all things. Hold on to what is good. Stay away from every kind of evil.
     1 Thessalonians 5:19–22

Now if any of you lacks wisdom, he should ask God—who gives to all generously and ungrudgingly—and it will be given to him.
    James 1:5

∞

Dear friends, do not believe every spirit, but test the spirits to see if they are from God, because many false prophets have gone out into the world.
    1 John 4:1

∞

Holy Spirit, may my spirit be open and receptive to Your prompting and leading so that I discern what is right and good in all things.

DISCOURAGEMENT

When our health is failing or we struggle to do the things we used to be able to do, we can rely on God to strengthen and uphold us.

∽

The LORD is the one who will go before you. He will be with you; he will not leave you or abandon you. Do not be afraid or discouraged.
        Deuteronomy 31:8

∽

"I have told you these things so that in me you may have peace. You will have suffering in this world. Be courageous! I have conquered the world."
        John 16:33

∽

Now may the God of hope fill you with all joy and peace as you believe so that you may overflow with hope by the power of the Holy Spirit.
        Romans 15:13

In the same way the Spirit also helps us in our weakness, because we do not know what to pray for as we should, but the Spirit himself intercedes for us with unspoken groanings. And he who searches our hearts knows the mind of the Spirit, because he intercedes for the saints according to the will of God. We know that all things work together for the good of those who love God, who are called according to his purpose.
    Romans 8:26–28

∽

But he said to me, "My grace is sufficient for you, for my power is perfected in weakness."
Therefore, I will most gladly boast all the more about my weaknesses, so that Christ's power may reside in me.
    2 Corinthians 12:9

∽

Lord, please grant me Your grace and strength
in this moment of discouragement.

DISSATISFIED

When we feel dissatisfied with our lives or circumstances, we can rediscover the abundance around us by practicing gratitude and thanksgiving.

❧

For he has satisfied the thirsty
and filled the hungry with good things.
    Psalm 107:9

❧

You open your hand
and satisfy the desire of every living thing.
    Psalm 145:16

❧

The LORD will always lead you, satisfy you in a parched land, and
strengthen your bones. You will be like a watered garden and like a
spring whose water never runs dry.
    Isaiah 58:11

"I am the bread of life," Jesus told them. "No one who comes to me will ever be hungry, and no one who believes in me will ever be thirsty again."

John 6:35

§

Now may the God of hope fill you with all joy and peace as you believe so that you may overflow with hope by the power of the Holy Spirit.

Romans 15:13

§

Dear God, no good thing do You withhold from Your people. Help me see the goodness all around me and to delight in Your good and perfect gifts.

ENCOURAGEMENT

As the psalmist says, this is the day that the Lord has made—rejoice and be glad in it!

❧

The LORD is the one who will go before you. He will be with you; he will not leave you or abandon you. Do not be afraid or discouraged.
Deuteronomy 31:8

❧

God is our refuge and strength,
a helper who is always found
in times of trouble.
Psalm 46:1

❧

"Aren't five sparrows sold for two pennies? Yet not one of them is forgotten in God's sight. Indeed, the hairs of your head are all counted. Don't be afraid; you are worth more than many sparrows."
Luke 12:6–7

I have told you these things so that in me you may have peace. You will have suffering in this world. Be courageous! I have conquered the world.
    John 16:33

❧

And let us watch out for one another to provoke love and good works, not neglecting to gather together, as some are in the habit of doing, but encouraging each other, and all the more as you see the day approaching.
    Hebrews 10:24–25

❧

Lord God, may Your Spirit strengthen and encourage my heart today, that I may be a source of encouragement for others.

ETERNITY

God knew you before He formed you in the womb, and you will be with Him throughout infinite life to come.

✍

Before the mountains were born,
before you gave birth to the earth and the world,
from eternity to eternity, you are God.
   Psalm 90:2

✍

He has made everything appropriate in its time. He has also put eternity
in their hearts, but no one can discover the work God has done from
beginning to end.
   Ecclesiastes 3:11

"Truly I tell you, anyone who hears my word and believes him who sent me has eternal life and will not come under judgment but has passed from death to life."
     John 5:24

❦

"This is eternal life: that they may know you, the only true God, and the one you have sent—Jesus Christ."
     John 17:3

❦

For the wages of sin is death, but the gift of God is eternal life in Christ Jesus our Lord.
     Romans 6:23

❦

Thank You, Father God, for the gift of eternal life through Your beloved Son.

FAILURE

Though failures of any kind can crush our spirits, we have the assurance that God's plans never fail.

∽

A person's steps are established by the LORD,
and he takes pleasure in his way.
Though he falls, he will not be overwhelmed,
because the LORD supports him with his hand.
    Psalm 37:23–24

∽

He brought me up from a desolate pit,
out of the muddy clay,
and set my feet on a rock,
making my steps secure.
He put a new song in my mouth,
a hymn of praise to our God.
Many will see and fear,
and they will trust in the LORD.
    Psalm 40:2–3

And not only that, but we also rejoice in our afflictions, because we know that affliction produces endurance, endurance produces proven character, and proven character produces hope.

Romans 5:3–4

ᴄᴊᴏ

Now we have this treasure in clay jars, so that this extraordinary power may be from God and not from us. We are afflicted in every way but not crushed; we are perplexed but not in despair; we are persecuted but not abandoned; we are struck down but not destroyed.

2 Corinthians 4:7–9

ᴄᴊᴏ

Brothers and sisters, I do not consider myself to have taken hold of it. But one thing I do: Forgetting what is behind and reaching forward to what is ahead, I pursue as my goal the prize promised by God's heavenly call in Christ Jesus.

Philippians 3:13–14

ᴄᴊᴏ

Heavenly Father, grant me grace in times of failure and help me press forward as I fix my eyes on Jesus.

FAITHFULNESS

God's everlasting faithfulness to His people is a deep source of hope, as well as an inspiration for how we should conduct ourselves in our relationships.

∽

Because of the LORD's faithful love
we do not perish,
for his mercies never end.
They are new every morning;
great is your faithfulness!
> *Lamentations 3:22–23*

∽

"His master said to him, 'Well done, good and faithful servant! You were faithful over a few things; I will put you in charge of many things. Share your master's joy.'"
> *Matthew 25:21*

"Whoever is faithful in very little is also faithful in much, and whoever is unrighteous in very little is also unrighteous in much. So if you have not been faithful with worldly wealth, who will trust you with what is genuine? And if you have not been faithful with what belongs to someone else, who will give you what is your own?"
Luke 16:10–12

∽

If we are faithless, he remains faithful, for he cannot deny himself.
2 Timothy 2:13

∽

Let us hold on to the confession of our hope without wavering, since he who promised is faithful.
Hebrews 10:23

∽

Dear God, whose mercies are new every morning, grant me wisdom to be faithful to my family, my church, and my community.

FAMILY

Grandparents are a precious source of love, wisdom, and encouragement for family members of all ages.

∽

This is why a man leaves his father and mother and bonds with his wife, and they become one flesh.
> *Genesis 2:24*

∽

"Honor your father and your mother so that you may have a long life in the land that the LORD your God is giving you."
> *Exodus 20:12*

∽

Fathers, don't stir up anger in your children, but bring them up in the training and instruction of the Lord.
> *Ephesians 6:4*

Sons are indeed a heritage from the LORD,
offspring, a reward.
Like arrows in the hand of a warrior
are the sons born in one's youth.
Happy is the man who has filled his quiver with them.
They will never be put to shame when they speak
with their enemies at the city gate.
　　　Psalm 127:3–5

⌇

Wives, submit to your husbands as to the Lord, because the husband is
the head of the wife as Christ is the head of the church. He is the Savior of
the body. Now as the church submits to Christ, so also wives are to submit
to their husbands in everything. Husbands, love your wives, just as Christ
loved the church and gave himself for her to make her holy, cleansing her
with the washing of water by the word. He did this to present the church
to himself in splendor, without spot or wrinkle or anything like that, but
holy and blameless. In the same way, husbands are to love their wives as
their own bodies. He who loves his wife loves himself.
　　　Ephesians 5:22–28

⌇

Lord, thank You for how You demonstrate Your love
and grace through my family and loved ones. May I
be a reflection of Your love to them in all I do and say.

FEAR

Most of our sense of dread comes not from an immediate threat but from fear of what might happen—but such false fear is unfounded; we have an almighty God who loves us and cares for us continually.

❧

"Haven't I commanded you: be strong and courageous? Do not be afraid or discouraged, for the LORD your God is with you wherever you go."
    Joshua 1:9

❧

When I am afraid,
I will trust in you.
    Psalm 56:3

❧

You did not receive a spirit of slavery to fall back into fear. Instead, you received the Spirit of adoption, by whom we cry out, "Abba, Father!"
    Romans 8:15

For God has not given us a spirit of fear, but one of power, love, and sound judgment.
    2 Timothy 1:7

࿇

Humble yourselves, therefore, under the mighty hand of God, so that he may exalt you at the proper time, casting all your cares on him, because he cares about you.
    1 Peter 5:6–7

࿇

Abba, Father, I cry out to You for Your protection and comfort in times when I'm afraid. Thank You for Your faithful love and comfort.

FELLOWSHIP

When our grown children and other family members are busy with their own lives, it's ever more important to avoid isolation and cultivate community.

❧

Iron sharpens iron,
and one person sharpens another.
    Proverbs 27:17

❧

Two are better than one because they have a good reward for their efforts. For if either falls, his companion can lift him up; but pity the one who falls without another to lift him up.
    Ecclesiastes 4:9–10

❧

Carry one another's burdens; in this way you will fulfill the law of Christ.
    Galatians 6:2

Therefore encourage one another and build each other up as you are already doing.

   1 Thessalonians 5:11

⨎

And let us watch out for one another to provoke love and good works, not neglecting to gather together, as some are in the habit of doing, but encouraging each other, and all the more as you see the day approaching.

   Hebrews 10:24–25

⨎

Dear Jesus, my heavenly Friend, please reveal to me ways I can spend more time in fellowship and build up others in my community.

FORGIVENESS

Forgiving someone who has wronged you means you no longer call to mind their fault or error—this extends grace to them and freedom for you.

❧

"*Therefore I tell you, her many sins have been forgiven; that's why she loved much. But the one who is forgiven little, loves little.*"
    Luke 7:47

❧

Live in harmony with one another. Do not be proud; instead, associate with the humble. Do not be wise in your own estimation. Do not repay anyone evil for evil. Give careful thought to do what is honorable in everyone's eyes. If possible, as far as it depends on you, live at peace with everyone.
    Romans 12:16–18

Be kind and compassionate to one another, forgiving one another, just as God also forgave you in Christ.

Ephesians 4:32

ᔆ

As God's chosen ones, holy and dearly loved, put on compassion, kindness, humility, gentleness, and patience, bearing with one another and forgiving one another if anyone has a grievance against another. Just as the Lord has forgiven you, so you are also to forgive.

Colossians 3:12–13

ᔆ

Dear God, just as You forgave all my debts and wrongs through Christ, empower me to extend forgiveness to anyone who has hurt me.

FRIENDSHIP

Precious are the people in our lives who have faithfully stood by us over decades of joys and sorrows, victories and failures, gains and loss.

෨

Iron sharpens iron,
and one person sharpens another.
    Proverbs 27:17

෨

Two are better than one because they have a good reward for their efforts. For if either falls, his companion can lift him up; but pity the one who falls without another to lift him up.
    Ecclesiastes 4:9–10

෨

Therefore encourage one another and build each other up as you are already doing.
    1 Thessalonians 5:11

"No one has greater love than this: to lay down his life for his friends. You are my friends if you do what I command you. I do not call you servants anymore, because a servant doesn't know what his master is doing. I have called you friends, because I have made known to you everything I have heard from my Father."
    John 15:13–15

⚭

Dear friends, let us love one another, because love is from God, and everyone who loves has been born of God and knows God.
    1 John 4:7

⚭

Lord Jesus, who called His disciples friends, thank You for demonstrating God's love for us and how best to love one another.

GENEROSITY

Generosity is about much more than giving away money—it's also about freely giving of your time, energy, and resources, knowing that all good things have been entrusted to you from the Lord.

✍

Good will come to the one who lends generously
and conducts his business fairly.
    Psalm 112:5

✍

"And if you lend to those from whom you expect to receive, what credit
is that to you? Even sinners lend to sinners to be repaid in full. But love
your enemies, do what is good, and lend, expecting nothing in return.
Then your reward will be great, and you will be children of the Most
High. For he is gracious to the ungrateful and evil."
    Luke 6:34–35

"Give, and it will be given to you; a good measure—pressed down, shaken together, and running over—will be poured into your lap. For with the measure you use, it will be measured back to you."
   Luke 6:38

❧

Each person should do as he has decided in his heart—not reluctantly or out of compulsion, since God loves a cheerful giver.
   2 Corinthians 9:7

❧

No one is to seek his own good, but the good of the other person.
   1 Corinthians 10:24

❧

Heavenly Father, who gives generously from His riches of grace in Christ Jesus, help me give freely from Your abundant blessings.

GENTLENESS

Gentleness is a gracious approach to others and a demeanor that reigns in strength or assertiveness.

❧

He protects his flock like a shepherd; he gathers the lambs in his arms and carries them in the fold of his garment. He gently leads those that are nursing.
Isaiah 40:11

❧

Let your graciousness be known to everyone. The Lord is near.
Philippians 4:5

The Lord's servant must not quarrel, but must be gentle to everyone, able to teach, and patient, instructing his opponents with gentleness.
   2 Timothy 2:24–25

⤫

Who among you is wise and understanding? By his good conduct he should show that his works are done in the gentleness that comes from wisdom.
   James 3:13

⤫

Lord Jesus, You are the Good Shepherd who demonstrates gentleness to Your people. May Your Spirit guide me in Your loving ways.

GRACE

The greatest gift we will ever receive is grace—the wholly unmerited favor of the Most High.

∾

The law came along to multiply the trespass. But where sin multiplied, grace multiplied even more.
Romans 5:20

∾

For sin will not rule over you, because you are not under the law but under grace.
Romans 6:14

∾

Now if by grace, then it is not by works; otherwise grace ceases to be grace.
Romans 11:6

But he said to me, "My grace is sufficient for you, for my power is perfected in weakness." Therefore, I will most gladly boast all the more about my weaknesses, so that Christ's power may reside in me.
     2 Corinthians 12:9

∽

For you are saved by grace through faith, and this is not from yourselves; it is God's gift—not from works, so that no one can boast.
     Ephesians 2:8–9

∽

Lord God, thank You for Your riches of grace that have been poured out on me through faith in Christ Jesus.

GREED

To hoard our possessions, money, food, or other blessings is to declare that there is not enough to go around—but God is faithful to provide for our needs.

❧

One person gives freely,
yet gains more;
another withholds what is right,
only to become poor.
     Proverbs 11:24

❧

A greedy person stirs up conflict,
but whoever trusts in the LORD will prosper.
     Proverbs 28:25

He then told them, "Watch out and be on guard against all greed, because one's life is not in the abundance of his possessions."
    Luke 12:15

∽

For the love of money is a root of all kinds of evil, and by craving it, some have wandered away from the faith and pierced themselves with many griefs.
    1 Timothy 6:10

∽

Keep your life free from the love of money. Be satisfied with what you have, for he himself has said, I will never leave you or abandon you.
    Hebrews 13:5

∽

Dear God, please forgive me of any lack of trust in Your provision, and make me a willing conduit of Your blessings and provision for those in need.

GRIEF

The deep sorrow of grief that comes from losing a loved one, a longtime friend, or even one's health can seem profound and unending—but God promises to be near us, to comfort us, and to bring joy and beauty out of the ashes.

ॐ

The righteous cry out, and the LORD hears,
and rescues them from all their troubles.
The LORD is near the brokenhearted;
he saves those crushed in spirit.
    Psalm 34:17–18

ॐ

Why, my soul, are you so dejected?
Why are you in such turmoil?
Put your hope in God, for I will still praise him,
my Savior and my God.
    Psalm 42:5

Then the young women will rejoice with dancing, while young and old men rejoice together. I will turn their mourning into joy, give them consolation, and bring happiness out of grief.
  Jeremiah 31:13

∽

Though the fig tree does not bud and there is no fruit on the vines, though the olive crop fails and the fields produce no food, though the flocks disappear from the pen and there are no herds in the stalls, yet I will celebrate in the Lord; I will rejoice in the God of my salvation!
  Habakkuk 3:17–18

∽

"So you also have sorrow now. But I will see you again. Your hearts will rejoice, and no one will take away your joy from you."
  John 16:22

∽

*Heavenly Father, when my heart is aching
and all I see is darkness, I trust that You are
my light and my salvation.*

GUILT

If we harm others or ourselves through willful or unintentional sin, we don't have to be consumed by guilt—because we know there is no condemnation for those in Christ Jesus.

❧

As far as the east is from the west,
so far has he removed
our transgressions from us.
  Psalm 103:12

❧

"Come, let us settle this,"
says the LORD.
"Though your sins are scarlet,
they will be as white as snow;
though they are crimson red,
they will be like wool."
  Isaiah 1:18

Therefore, there is now no condemnation for those in Christ Jesus, because the law of the Spirit of life in Christ Jesus has set you free from the law of sin and death.
Romans 8:1–2

✍

In him we have redemption through his blood, the forgiveness of our trespasses, according to the riches of his grace.
Ephesians 1:7

✍

If we confess our sins, he is faithful and righteous to forgive us our sins and to cleanse us from all unrighteousness.
1 John 1:9

✍

Lord, when I have fallen short of Your glory, grant me the wisdom to confess my sins and be cleansed of all unrighteousness.

HAPPINESS

Though happiness sometimes comes from external circumstances, we experience the most lasting happiness by enjoying our union with Christ.

❧

Therefore my heart is glad
and my whole being rejoices;
my body also rests securely.
  Psalm 16:9

❧

Take delight in the LORD,
and he will give you your heart's desires.
  Psalm 37:4

A joyful heart makes a face cheerful,
but a sad heart produces a broken spirit.
    Proverbs 15:13

❧

I know that there is nothing better for them than to rejoice and enjoy the
good life.
    Ecclesiastes 3:12

❧

Rejoice in the Lord always. I will say it again: Rejoice!
    Philippians 4:4

❧

Lord Jesus, may my heart be happy
and cheerful because I know You.

HEALTH

The decline of good health is a discouraging aspect of aging, but through good health habits and God's grace, we can remain strong for many years.

❧

My flesh and my heart may fail,
but God is the strength of my heart,
my portion forever.
      Psalm 73:26

❧

He heals the brokenhearted
and bandages their wounds.
      Psalm 147:3

❧

So, whether you eat or drink, or whatever you do, do everything for the glory of God.
      1 Corinthians 10:31

Don't be wise in your own eyes;
fear the LORD and turn away from evil.
This will be healing for your body
and strengthening for your bones.
> *Proverbs 3:7–8*

✍

Don't you know that your body is a temple of the Holy Spirit who is in
you, whom you have from God? You are not your own, for you were
bought at a price. So glorify God with your body.
> *1 Corinthians 6:19–20*

✍

Dear God, grant me wisdom for ways
to strengthen this temple of the Holy Spirit
and give me strength for this day.

HEAVEN

Our greatest hope is enjoying the eternal, constant presence of the Lord Jesus for all eternity—where there will be no more sorrow or pain.

❧

"Sell your possessions and give to the poor. Make money-bags for yourselves that won't grow old, an inexhaustible treasure in heaven, where no thief comes near and no moth destroys. For where your treasure is, there your heart will be also."
    Luke 12:33–34

❧

Then one of the criminals hanging there began to yell insults at him: "Aren't you the Messiah? Save yourself and us!"
    But the other answered, rebuking him: "Don't you even fear God, since you are undergoing the same punishment? We are punished justly, because we're getting back what we deserve for the things we did, but this man has done nothing wrong." Then he said, "Jesus, remember me when you come into your kingdom." And he said to him, "Truly I tell you, today you will be with me in paradise."
    Luke 23:39–43

"In my Father's house are many rooms; if not, I would have told you. I am going away to prepare a place for you."

John 14:2

❧

But as it is written, What no eye has seen, no ear has heard, and no human heart has conceived—God has prepared these things for those who love him.

1 Corinthians 2:9

❧

He will wipe away every tear from their eyes. Death will be no more; grief, crying, and pain will be no more, because the previous things have passed away.

Revelation 21:4

❧

Thank you, heavenly Father, for making a way to enjoy you forever, and help me to live daily with this hope.

HONOR

Our culture tends to be informal and irreverent, but as believers, we can stand apart by showing honor and respect to everyone we encounter.

❧

Honor the LORD with your possessions
and with the first produce of your entire harvest;
then your barns will be completely filled,
and your vats will overflow with new wine.
    Proverbs 3:9–10

❧

Now to the King eternal, immortal, invisible, the only God, be honor
and glory forever and ever. Amen.
    1 Timothy 1:17

Pray for us, for we are convinced that we have a clear conscience, wanting to conduct ourselves honorably in everything.
Hebrews 13:18

⚬

Honor everyone. Love the brothers and sisters. Fear God. Honor the emperor.
1 Peter 2:17

⚬

Lord God, may Your Spirit guide me to honor You
with my speech, actions, time, and resources.

HOPE

It's tempting to put our hope in the wrong places—retirement funds, family members, personal abilities—but our firmest hope is found only in Christ Jesus.

⁑

But those who trust in the LORD
will renew their strength;
they will soar on wings like eagles;
they will run and not become weary,
they will walk and not faint.
    Isaiah 40:31

⁑

Let us run with endurance the race that lies before us, keeping our eyes on Jesus, the source and perfecter of our faith. For the joy that lay before him, he endured the cross, despising the shame, and sat down at the right hand of the throne of God. For consider him who endured such hostility from sinners against himself, so that you won't grow weary and give up.
    Hebrews 12:1–3

I wait for the LORD; I wait
and put my hope in his word.
        Psalm 130:5

 озн

We have also obtained access through him by faith into this grace in
which we stand, and we rejoice in the hope of the glory of God. And not
only that, but we also rejoice in our afflictions, because we know that
affliction produces endurance, endurance produces proven character,
and proven character produces hope.
        Romans 5:2–4

озн

Now may the God of hope fill you with all joy and peace as you believe
so that you may overflow with hope by the power of the Holy Spirit.
        Romans 15:13

озн

Lord of hope, please fill me with joy
and peace as I hope in You.

HUMILITY

The key to cultivating true humility isn't to act self-deprecating but to simply not think of oneself much at all.

℁

Sitting down, he called the Twelve and said to them, "If anyone wants to be first, he must be last and servant of all."
   Mark 9:35

℁

Live in harmony with one another. Do not be proud; instead, associate with the humble. Do not be wise in your own estimation.
   Romans 12:16

℁

Do nothing out of selfish ambition or conceit, but in humility consider others as more important than yourselves.
   Philippians 2:3

Adopt the same attitude as that of Christ Jesus, who, existing in the form of God, did not consider equality with God as something to be exploited. Instead he emptied himself by assuming the form of a servant, taking on the likeness of humanity. And when he had come as a man, he humbled himself by becoming obedient to the point of death—even to death on a cross.

Philippians 2:5–8

❧

Who among you is wise and understanding? By his good conduct he should show that his works are done in the gentleness that comes from wisdom.

James 3:13

❧

Lord Jesus, who demonstrated perfect selflessness, please fill my mind with thoughts of You and of others so that I forget myself completely.

INTEGRITY

The late basketball coach John Wooden once said, "The true test of a person's character is what he does when no one is watching."

∽

The one who lives with integrity lives securely,
but whoever perverts his ways will be found out.
Proverbs 10:9

∽

Better the poor person who lives with integrity
than the rich one who distorts right and wrong.
Proverbs 28:6

∽

Indeed, we are giving careful thought to do what is right, not only before
the Lord but also before people.
2 Corinthians 8:21

*Whatever you do, do it from the heart, as something done for the Lord
and not for people, knowing that you will receive the reward of an
inheritance from the Lord. You serve the Lord Christ.*
    Colossians 3:23–24

⁓

*Yet do this with gentleness and respect, keeping a clear conscience, so
that when you are accused, those who disparage your good conduct in
Christ will be put to shame.*
    1 Peter 3:16

⁓

*Search me, Lord God and know my heart,
and if there is anything ungodly in me,
lead me in the way everlasting.*

JOY

Happiness can be fleeting, but joy is steadfast because it is a state of being rooted in our soul's intimacy with Christ.

❧

You reveal the path of life to me;
in your presence is abundant joy;
at your right hand are eternal pleasures.
　　　Psalm 16:11

❧

This is the day the LORD has made;
let us rejoice and be glad in it.
　　　Psalm 118:24

But the fruit of the Spirit is love, joy, peace, patience, kindness, goodness, faithfulness, gentleness, and self-control. The law is not against such things.

Galatians 5:22–23

❧

"As the Father has loved me, I have also loved you. Remain in my love. If you keep my commands you will remain in my love, just as I have kept my Father's commands and remain in his love. I have told you these things so that my joy may be in you and your joy may be complete."

John 15:9–11

❧

Heavenly Father, thank You for your faithfulness and that in Your presence is abundant joy.

JUSTICE

God's Word makes it clear how deeply He cares about the poor and the oppressed, and He calls us to act accordingly.

∽

Do not act unjustly when deciding a case. Do not be partial to the poor or give preference to the rich; judge your neighbor fairly.
    Leviticus 19:15

∽

Isn't this the fast I choose: To break the chains of wickedness, to untie the ropes of the yoke, to set the oppressed free, and to tear off every yoke? Is it not to share your bread with the hungry, to bring the poor and homeless into your house, to clothe the naked when you see him, and not to ignore your own flesh and blood?
    Isaiah 58:6–7

The LORD of Armies says this: "Make fair decisions. Show faithful love and compassion to one another. Do not oppress the widow or the fatherless, the resident alien or the poor, and do not plot evil in your hearts against one another."
Zechariah 7:9–10

☙

Don't be deceived: God is not mocked. For whatever a person sows he will also reap,
Galatians 6:7

☙

Pure and undefiled religion before God the Father is this: to look after orphans and widows in their distress and to keep oneself unstained from the world.
James 1:27

☙

Father God, please open my eyes and heart to the needs in my community and empower me to bring Your light to dark corners.

KINDNESS

In God's great kindness, He saved us through His beloved Son, and He now calls us to extend that same gentleness and compassion to others.

ℭ

He also raised us up with him and seated us with him in the heavens in Christ Jesus, so that in the coming ages he might display the immeasurable riches of his grace through his kindness to us in Christ Jesus.

Ephesians 2:6–7

ℭ

Let all bitterness, anger and wrath, shouting and slander be removed from you, along with all malice. And be kind and compassionate to one another, forgiving one another, just as God also forgave you in Christ.

Ephesians 4:31–32

Therefore, as God's chosen ones, holy and dearly loved, put on compassion, kindness, humility, gentleness, and patience.
    Colossians 3:12

∽

But when the kindness of God our Savior and his love for mankind appeared, he saved us—not by works of righteousness that we had done, but according to his mercy—through the washing of regeneration and renewal by the Holy Spirit.
    Titus 3:4–6

∽

Dear God, may Your Holy Spirit soften my speech and actions so that I display Your kindness to those I encounter today.

KNOWLEDGE

Though you have a lifetime of knowledge and experience, the truest knowledge is having awe and reverence for the Creator.

❧

For wisdom will enter your heart,
and knowledge will delight you.
> *Proverbs 2:10*

❧

The mind of the discerning acquires knowledge,
and the ear of the wise seeks it.
> *Proverbs 18:15*

❧

For the earth will be filled with the knowledge of the LORD's glory, as the
water covers the sea.
> *Habakkuk 2:14*

We know that "we all have knowledge." Knowledge puffs up, but love builds up. If anyone thinks he knows anything, he does not yet know it as he ought to know it. But if anyone loves God, he is known by him.
    1 Corinthians 8:1–3

∽

For this reason also, since the day we heard this, we haven't stopped praying for you. We are asking that you may be filled with the knowledge of his will in all wisdom and spiritual understanding, so that you may walk worthy of the Lord, fully pleasing to him: bearing fruit in every good work and growing in the knowledge of God, being strengthened with all power, according to his glorious might, so that you may have great endurance and patience, joyfully giving thanks to the Father, who has enabled you to share in the saints' inheritance in the light.
    Colossians 1:9–12

∽

*Lord, may Your Spirit teach me Your Word
and guide me in Your perfect ways.*

LONELINESS

The older we get, the easier it is to become isolated—but thanks to God's faithful presence and our community of believers, we never have to be alone.

⌘

"My presence will go with you, and I will give you rest."
  Exodus 33:14

⌘

The LORD is the one who will go before you. He will be with you; he will not leave you or abandon you. Do not be afraid or discouraged.
  Deuteronomy 31:8

⌘

God provides homes for those who are deserted.
He leads out the prisoners to prosperity,
but the rebellious live in a scorched land.
  Psalm 68:6

He heals the brokenhearted
and bandages their wounds.
Psalm 147:3

⚭

Blessed be the God and Father of our Lord Jesus Christ, the Father of mercies and the God of all comfort. He comforts us in all our affliction, so that we may be able to comfort those who are in any kind of affliction, through the comfort we ourselves receive from God.
2 Corinthians 1:3–4

⚭

Father of mercies, please comfort me in times of loneliness so I may be a comfort to others.

LOVE

Our highest calling is to love God with all of our heart, our soul, and our mind, and to love our neighbor as ourselves.

∽

"But I say to you who listen: Love your enemies, do what is good to those who hate you, bless those who curse you, pray for those who mistreat you."
    Luke 6:27–28

∽

Love is patient, love is kind. Love does not envy, is not boastful, is not arrogant, is not rude, is not self-seeking, is not irritable, and does not keep a record of wrongs.
    1 Corinthians 13:4–5

Above all, maintain constant love for one another, since love covers a multitude of sins.

1 Peter 4:8

∽

God's love was revealed among us in this way: God sent his one and only Son into the world so that we might live through him.

1 John 4:9

∽

And we have come to know and to believe the love that God has for us. God is love, and the one who remains in love remains in God, and God remains in him.

1 John 4:16

∽

Dear Jesus, instill in my heart the kind of selfless concern for the well-being of others that You demonstrated for us.

MERCY

When you feel that life is too much to take, remember that you can approach God's throne of grace with boldness.

_∽_

"Blessed are the merciful, for they will be shown mercy."
    Matthew 5:7

_∽_

"Go and learn what this means: I desire mercy and not sacrifice. For I didn't come to call the righteous, but sinners."
    Matthew 9:13

_∽_

Therefore, let us approach the throne of grace with boldness, so that we may receive mercy and find grace to help us in time of need.
    Hebrews 4:16

Speak and act as those who are to be judged by the law of freedom. For judgment is without mercy to the one who has not shown mercy. Mercy triumphs over judgment.

   James 2:12–13

cℓℓ

Blessed be the God and Father of our Lord Jesus Christ. Because of his great mercy he has given us new birth into a living hope through the resurrection of Jesus Christ from the dead.

   1 Peter 1:3

cℓℓ

Lord God, thank You for Your mercy
and grace in times of need.

OBEDIENCE

Obedience to God means yielding our will to His, and His will is that we love Him and our neighbor as ourselves—on these two commandments depend all the law and the prophets.

∽

I have chosen the way of truth;
I have set your ordinances before me.
    Psalm 119:30

∽

"If you love me, you will keep my commands."
    John 14:15

∽

Peter and the apostles replied, "We must obey God rather than people."
    Acts 5:29

The one who keeps his commands remains in him, and he in him. And the way we know that he remains in us is from the Spirit he has given us.
    1 John 3:24

✍

For this is what love for God is: to keep his commands. And his commands are not a burden, because everyone who has been born of God conquers the world. This is the victory that has conquered the world: our faith.
    1 John 5:3–4

✍

Lord Jesus, may Your Spirit guide me in all my thoughts, words, and actions that I may be fully submitted to Your will.

PATIENCE

When we are impatient in our actions or behavior, we risk making wrong choices or damaging our relationships.

∽

The end of a matter is better than its beginning;
a patient spirit is better than a proud spirit.
    Ecclesiastes 7:8

∽

Now if we hope for what we do not see, we eagerly wait for it with patience.
    Romans 8:25

∽

My dear brothers and sisters, understand this: Everyone should be quick to listen, slow to speak, and slow to anger, for human anger does not accomplish God's righteousness.
    James 1:19–20

Therefore, brothers and sisters, be patient until the Lord's coming. See how the farmer waits for the precious fruit of the earth and is patient with it until it receives the early and the late rains. You also must be patient. Strengthen your hearts, because the Lord's coming is near.

James 5:7–8

❧

The Lord does not delay his promise, as some understand delay, but is patient with you, not wanting any to perish but all to come to repentance.

2 Peter 3:9

❧

Heavenly Father, You are patient and slow to anger; please help me be still and wait patiently for You.

PEACE

The way to peace is to quiet the ruminating mind, which worries over what has happened in the past and what might happen in the future.

⚮

You will keep the mind that is dependent on you in perfect peace, for it is trusting in you.
Isaiah 26:3

⚮

And the peace of God, which surpasses all understanding, will guard your hearts and minds in Christ Jesus. Finally brothers and sisters, whatever is true, whatever is honorable, whatever is just, whatever is pure, whatever is lovely, whatever is commendable—if there is any moral excellence and if there is anything praiseworthy—dwell on these things.
Philippians 4:7–8

"Peace I leave with you. My peace I give to you. I do not give to you as the world gives. Don't let your heart be troubled or fearful."
  John 14:27

         ↄʃoↄ

For I am persuaded that neither death nor life, nor angels nor rulers, nor things present nor things to come, nor powers, nor height nor depth, nor any other created thing will be able to separate us from the love of God that is in Christ Jesus our Lord.
  Romans 8:38–39

         ↄʃoↄ

*Lord Jesus, may Your perfect peace guard
my heart and mind as I trust in You.*

PERSEVERANCE

No matter what trial you face or how exhausted you may feel, remember that the Lord upholds you and strengthens you at all times.

∽

And not only that, but we also rejoice in our afflictions, because we know that affliction produces endurance, endurance produces proven character, and proven character produces hope. This hope will not disappoint us, because God's love has been poured out in our hearts through the Holy Spirit who was given to us.
    Romans 5:3–5

∽

Let us not get tired of doing good, for we will reap at the proper time if we don't give up.
    Galatians 6:9

Therefore, since we also have such a large cloud of witnesses surrounding us, let us lay aside every hindrance and the sin that so easily ensnares us. Let us run with endurance the race that lies before us, keeping our eyes on Jesus, the source and perfecter of our faith. For the joy that lay before him, he endured the cross, despising the shame, and sat down at the right hand of the throne of God.

   Hebrews 12:1–2

∽

Consider it a great joy, my brothers and sisters, whenever you experience various trials, because you know that the testing of your faith produces endurance. And let endurance have its full effect, so that you may be mature and complete, lacking nothing.

   James 1:2–4

∽

Blessed is the one who endures trials, because when he has stood the test he will receive the crown of life that God has promised to those who love him.

   James 1:12

∽

Dear Jesus, help me fix my eyes on You that Your Spirit may strengthen my heart and will to persevere.

PRAYER

No matter how we come to the Lord, whether to present our requests and needs or to sit silently in His presence, we can trust that He hears us.

∽

"Whenever you pray, you must not be like the hypocrites, because they love to pray standing in the synagogues and on the street corners to be seen by people. Truly I tell you, they have their reward. But when you pray, go into your private room, shut your door, and pray to your Father who is in secret. And your Father who sees in secret will reward you. When you pray, don't babble like the Gentiles, since they imagine they'll be heard for their many words. Don't be like them, because your Father knows the things you need before you ask him.

"Therefore, you should pray like this: Our Father in heaven, your name be honored as holy. Your kingdom come. Your will be done on earth as it is in heaven. Give us today our daily bread. And forgive us our debts, as we also have forgiven our debtors. And do not bring us into temptation, but deliver us from the evil one.

"For if you forgive others their offenses, your heavenly Father will forgive you as well. But if you don't forgive others, your Father will not forgive your offenses."

Matthew 6:5–15

"If you remain in me and my words remain in you, ask whatever you want and it will be done for you."

John 15:7

∽

In the same way the Spirit also helps us in our weakness, because we do not know what to pray for as we should, but the Spirit himself intercedes for us with unspoken groanings.

Romans 8:26

∽

Don't worry about anything, but in everything, through prayer and petition with thanksgiving, present your requests to God.

Philippians 4:6

∽

Pray constantly.

1 Thessalonians 5:17

∽

Lord Jesus, just as You taught Your followers how to pray, instill in me a deep desire to seek Your presence.

PRIDE

With age often comes wisdom and success, but we can avoid arrogance by remembering that all good things have come by the grace of God.

∽

When arrogance comes, disgrace follows,
but with humility comes wisdom.
    Proverbs 11:2

∽

Everyone with a proud heart is detestable to the LORD;
be assured, he will not go unpunished.
    Proverbs 16:5

∽

A person's pride will humble him,
but a humble spirit will gain honor.
    Proverbs 29:23

Live in harmony with one another. Do not be proud; instead, associate with the humble. Do not be wise in your own estimation.

Romans 12:16

∽

For if anyone considers himself to be something when he is nothing, he deceives himself.

Galatians 6:3

∽

Lord God, please forgive the ways I puff myself up rather than humble myself under Your loving hand.

PROTECTION

Our security and peace comes from the Lord, who is our strong tower and refuge.

∽

Protect me as the pupil of your eye;
hide me in the shadow of your wings
     Psalm 17:8

∽

The angel of the LORD encamps
around those who fear him, and rescues them.
     Psalm 34:7

∽

The mountains surround Jerusalem
and the LORD surrounds his people,
both now and forever.
     Psalm 125:2

The name of the LORD is a strong tower;
the righteous run to it and are protected.
    Proverbs 18:10

∽

But the Lord is faithful; he will strengthen and guard you from the evil
one.
    2 Thessalonians 3:3

∽

Heavenly Father, please watch over me,
my family, our children, and grandchildren,
according to Your mercy and grace.

PURPOSE

Our deepest purpose is not in what we do but in who we are—people who love, honor, and praise God.

❧

Sing to him; sing praise to him; tell about all his wondrous works! Honor his holy name; let the hearts of those who seek the LORD rejoice.
    1 Chronicles 16:9–10

❧

When all has been heard, the conclusion of the matter is this: fear God and keep his commands, because this is for all humanity.
    Ecclesiastes 12:13

❧

"My Father is glorified by this: that you produce much fruit and prove to be my disciples."
    John 15:8

But I consider my life of no value to myself; my purpose is to finish my course and the ministry I received from the Lord Jesus, to testify to the gospel of God's grace.
    Acts 20:24

∽

He has saved us and called us with a holy calling, not according to our works, but according to his own purpose and grace, which was given to us in Christ Jesus before time began.
    2 Timothy 1:9

∽

Lord Jesus, may each day offer me opportunities to live out my true purpose by loving and serving You and those around me.

RELATIONSHIPS

Loving relationships and friendships are gifts from God—we are built up and supported in community and in fellowship with other believers.

❦

Then the LORD God said, "It is not good for the man to be alone. I will make a helper corresponding to him."
    Genesis 2:18

❦

But if they do not have self-control, they should marry, since it is better to marry than to burn with desire.
    1 Corinthians 7:9

❦

Don't become partners with those who do not believe. For what partnership is there between righteousness and lawlessness? Or what fellowship does light have with darkness?
    2 Corinthians 6:14

Therefore encourage one another and build each other up as you are already doing.
    1 Thessalonians 5:11

⨕

Above all, maintain constant love for one another, since love covers a multitude of sins.
    1 Peter 4:8

⨕

Heavenly Father, reveal to me ways I can be a conduit of Your love toward those in my community today.

RELIABILITY

Grandparents are often a family's most steadfast source of support—as believers, we can stand apart by being dependable and committed to our word.

∽

He will not allow your foot to slip;
your Protector will not slumber.
    Psalm 121:3

∽

"But let your 'yes' mean 'yes,' and your 'no' mean 'no.' Anything more
than this is from the evil one."
    Matthew 5:37

"Whoever is faithful in very little is also faithful in much, and whoever is unrighteous in very little is also unrighteous in much."
Luke 16:10

∽

What you have heard from me in the presence of many witnesses, commit to faithful men who will be able to teach others also.
2 Timothy 2:2

∽

Lord, just as You are constant and faithful, help me to be someone others can reliably depend upon.

RIGHTEOUSNESS

Praise be to God, who made the one who knew no sin to be sin for us, so that in Him we might become the very righteousness of God.

❦

How happy are those who uphold justice,
who practice righteousness at all times.
> *Psalm 106:3*

❦

"For I tell you, unless your righteousness surpasses that of the scribes and Pharisees, you will never get into the kingdom of heaven."
> *Matthew 5:20*

❦

He made the one who did not know sin to be sin for us, so that in him we might become the righteousness of God.
> *2 Corinthians 5:21*

But even if you should suffer for righteousness, you are blessed. Do not fear what they fear or be intimidated, but in your hearts regard Christ the Lord as holy, ready at any time to give a defense to anyone who asks you for a reason for the hope that is in you.

1 Peter 3:14–15

ℚ

Children, let no one deceive you. The one who does what is right is righteous, just as he is righteous.

1 John 3:7

ℚ

*Heavenly Father, may Your Spirit
guide me and empower me to glorify
You by doing what is right and just.*

SAVIOR

Christ Jesus is our Savior, the Source and Perfector of our faith, who for the joy set before Him endured the cross.

ॐ

He said, "They are indeed my people, children who will not be disloyal," and he became their Savior. In all their suffering, he suffered, and the angel of his presence saved them. He redeemed them because of his love and compassion; he lifted them up and carried them all the days of the past.
　　Isaiah 63:8–9

ॐ

My soul praises the greatness of the Lord, and my spirit rejoices in God my Savior, because he has looked with favor on the humble condition of his servant.
　　Luke 1:46–48

"This Jesus is the stone rejected by you builders, which has become the cornerstone. There is salvation in no one else, for there is no other name under heaven given to people by which we must be saved."

Acts 4:11–12

❧

This is good, and it pleases God our Savior, who wants everyone to be saved and to come to the knowledge of the truth.

1 Timothy 2:3–4

❧

And we have seen and we testify that the Father has sent his Son as the world's Savior.

1 John 4:14

❧

Lord Jesus, I have been crucified with You—
may the life I now live be lived for You who
loved me and gave Yourself for me.

SERVICE

Since Jesus, the King of Heaven, came not to be served but to serve others, we should seek to love others in the same way.

⁓

"And the King will answer them, 'Truly I tell you, whatever you did for one of the least of these brothers and sisters of mine, you did for me.'"
  Matthew 25:40

⁓

"For even the Son of Man did not come to be served, but to serve, and to give his life as a ransom for many."
  Mark 10:45

I have been crucified with Christ, and I no longer live, but Christ lives in me. The life I now live in the body, I live by faith in the Son of God, who loved me and gave himself for me.

Galatians 2:20

❦

Therefore, my dear brothers and sisters, be steadfast, immovable, always excelling in the Lord's work, because you know that your labor in the Lord is not in vain.

1 Corinthians 15:58

❦

Lord Jesus, please open my eyes and heart to freely and joyously respond to the needs of others today.

SOVEREIGNTY OF GOD

We trust in God's sovereignty because He is the Creator of the universe and sustains all things by His powerful Word.

〜

The LORD does whatever he pleases
in heaven and on earth,
in the seas and all the depths.
        Psalm 135:6

〜

A person's heart plans his way,
but the LORD determines his steps.
        Proverbs 16:9

〜

A king's heart is like channeled water in the LORD's hand:
He directs it wherever he chooses.
        Proverbs 21:1

What should we say then? Is there injustice with God? Absolutely not! For he tells Moses, I will show mercy to whom I will show mercy, and I will have compassion on whom I will have compassion. So then, it does not depend on human will or effort but on God who shows mercy. For the Scripture tells Pharaoh, I raised you up for this reason so that I may display my power in you and that my name may be proclaimed in the whole earth. So then, he has mercy on whom he wants to have mercy and he hardens whom he wants to harden.

Romans 9:14–18

∽

We know that all things work together for the good of those who love God, who are called according to his purpose.

Romans 8:28

∽

My good and faithful God, may my heart and soul rest in knowing that You uphold the world and Your purposes cannot be thwarted.

SPEECH

When we speak, the words we choose are only part of our response—we must also consider our motives and tone of voice.

✀

A gentle answer turns away anger,
but a harsh word stirs up wrath.
        Proverbs 15:1

✀

Let your speech always be gracious, seasoned with salt, so that you may know how you should answer each person.
        Colossians 4:6

✀

Bless those who persecute you; bless and do not curse.
        Romans 12:14

But no one can tame the tongue. It is a restless evil, full of deadly poison. With the tongue we bless our Lord and Father, and with it we curse people who are made in God's likeness. Blessing and cursing come out of the same mouth. My brothers and sisters, these things should not be this way.

James 3:8–10

❦

No foul language should come from your mouth, but only what is good for building up someone in need, so that it gives grace to those who hear.

Ephesians 4:29

❦

Holy Spirit, please fill my heart with the gracious love of God so that my speech is humble, gentle, and kind.

SUCCESS

Whether you succeed or fail at your endeavors, your true identity is your relationship with the Lord Jesus.

❧

Take delight in the LORD,
and he will give you your heart's desires.
    Psalm 37:4

❧

Commit your activities to the LORD,
and your plans will be established.
    Proverbs 16:3

"For what will it benefit someone if he gains the whole world yet loses his life? Or what will anyone give in exchange for his life? For the Son of Man is going to come with his angels in the glory of his Father, and then he will reward each according to what he has done."

Matthew 16:26–27

✎

Humble yourselves before the Lord, and he will exalt you.

James 4:10

✎

Lord Jesus, no matter how well I do in life, help me remember that my purpose is to be a shining beacon of Your light and love.

TEACHING

As wise and mature adults, we have the opportunity to teach the rising generations the blessed ways of the Lord.

∽

Until I come, give your attention to public reading, exhortation, and teaching.
    1 Timothy 4:13

∽

Preach the word; be ready in season and out of season; rebuke, correct, and encourage with great patience and teaching.
    2 Timothy 4:2

∽

Not many should become teachers, my brothers, because you know that we will receive a stricter judgment.
    James 3:1

In the same way, encourage the young men to be self-controlled in everything. Make yourself an example of good works with integrity and dignity in your teaching. Your message is to be sound beyond reproach, so that any opponent will be ashamed, because he doesn't have anything bad to say about us.

Titus 2:6–8

⤨

Heavenly Father, as You have taught me through Your Word, may I be a source of godly instruction for the younger people in my life.

TEMPTATION

There are some temptations that are unavoidable, however God is faithful to provide an escape from what tempts you.

∽

"Stay awake and pray, so that you won't enter into temptation. The spirit is willing, but the flesh is weak."
    Matthew 26:41

∽

No temptation has come upon you except what is common to humanity. But God is faithful; he will not allow you to be tempted beyond what you are able, but with the temptation he will also provide a way out so that you may be able to bear it.
    1 Corinthians 10:13

For since he himself has suffered when he was tempted, he is able to help those who are tempted.
    Hebrews 2:18

⌘

No one undergoing a trial should say, "I am being tempted by God," since God is not tempted by evil, and he himself doesn't tempt anyone. But each person is tempted when he is drawn away and enticed by his own evil desire. Then after desire has conceived, it gives birth to sin, and when sin is fully grown, it gives birth to death.
    James 1:13–15

⌘

Therefore, submit to God. Resist the devil, and he will flee from you.
    James 4:7

⌘

*Lord God, my spirit is willing, but my flesh is weak—
please help me to honor You in all of my choices.*

THANKFULNESS

The more we practice gratitude and thanksgiving, the more abundance and goodness we recognize all around us.

❧

Give thanks to the LORD, for he is good;
his faithful love endures forever.
    Psalm 118:1

❧

For we know that the one who raised the Lord Jesus will also raise us with Jesus and present us with you. Indeed, everything is for your benefit so that, as grace extends through more and more people, it may cause thanksgiving to increase to the glory of God.
    2 Corinthians 4:14–16

Let the word of Christ dwell richly among you, in all wisdom teaching and admonishing one another through psalms, hymns, and spiritual songs, singing to God with gratitude in your hearts.
Colossians 3:16

∽

Rejoice always, pray constantly, give thanks in everything; for this is God's will for you in Christ Jesus.
1 Thessalonians 5:16–18

∽

Every good and perfect gift is from above, coming down from the Father of lights, who does not change like shifting shadows.
James 1:17

∽

Father of lights, I praise You and thank You for every good and perfect gift You have given.

TRUST

To trust the Lord is to believe what He has said about Himself: He is good, faithful, and sovereign.

∽

The person who trusts in the LORD, whose confidence indeed is the LORD, is blessed. He will be like a tree planted by water: it sends its roots out toward a stream, it doesn't fear when heat comes, and its foliage remains green. It will not worry in a year of drought or cease producing fruit.

Jeremiah 17:7–8

∽

Wait for the LORD;
be strong, and let your heart be courageous.
Wait for the LORD.

Psalm 27:14

I will be with you when you pass through the waters, and when you pass through the rivers, they will not overwhelm you. You will not be scorched when you walk through the fire, and the flame will not burn you.

    Isaiah 43:2

∽

And my God will supply all your needs according to his riches in glory in Christ Jesus.

    Philippians 4:19

∽

This is the confidence we have before him: If we ask anything according to his will, he hears us.

    1 John 5:14

∽

Dear God, thank You that all things work together for the good of those who love You and are called according to Your purpose.

WEALTH

God has provided richly for us with things to enjoy; therefore let us be gracious and generous toward those in need.

❧

Who do I have in heaven but you?
And I desire nothing on earth but you.
      Psalm 73:25

❧

"Don't store up for yourselves treasures on earth, where moth and rust destroy and where thieves break in and steal. But store up for yourselves treasures in heaven, where neither moth nor rust destroys, and where thieves don't break in and steal."
      Matthew 6:19–20

I know both how to make do with little, and I know how to make do with a lot. In any and all circumstances I have learned the secret of being content—whether well fed or hungry, whether in abundance or in need.
    Philippians 4:12

❧

Instruct those who are rich in the present age not to be arrogant or to set their hope on the uncertainty of wealth, but on God, who richly provides us with all things to enjoy. Instruct them to do what is good, to be rich in good works, to be generous and willing to share, storing up treasure for themselves as a good foundation for the coming age, so that they may take hold of what is truly life.
    1 Timothy 6:17–19

❧

*Lord Jesus, I praise You and thank You that
my richest gain is knowing You.*

WISDOM

Though we may have a lifetime of experience, true wisdom comes from the Holy Spirit, who helps us discern what is true, good, and right.

✎

Teach us to number our days carefully
so that we may develop wisdom in our hearts.
    Psalm 90:12

✎

Do not be conformed to this age, but be transformed by the renewing
of your mind, so that you may discern what is the good, pleasing, and
perfect will of God.
    Romans 12:2

Yet to those who are called, both Jews and Greeks, Christ is the power of God and the wisdom of God, because God's foolishness is wiser than human wisdom, and God's weakness is stronger than human strength.
     1 Corinthians 1:24–25

cχ∕ο

Now if any of you lacks wisdom, he should ask God—who gives to all generously and ungrudgingly—and it will be given to him.
     James 1:5

cχ∕ο

Heavenly Father, who gives generously and ungrudgingly, please fill me with Your wisdom.

WORRY

Worry is false and useless fear: it's imagining and anticipating what might happen but probably won't.

❧

"Therefore I tell you: Don't worry about your life, what you will eat or what you will drink; or about your body, what you will wear. Isn't life more than food and the body more than clothing? Consider the birds of the sky: They don't sow or reap or gather into barns, yet your heavenly Father feeds them. Aren't you worth more than they? Can any of you add one moment to his life-span by worrying?"
    Matthew 6:25–27

❧

The Lord answered her, "Martha, Martha, you are worried and upset about many things, but one thing is necessary. Mary has made the right choice, and it will not be taken away from her."
    Luke 10:41–42

We know that all things work together for the good of those who love God, who are called according to his purpose.
    Romans 8:28

∽

Don't worry about anything, but in everything, through prayer and petition with thanksgiving, present your requests to God. And the peace of God, which surpasses all understanding, will guard your hearts and minds in Christ Jesus.
    Philippians 4:6–7

∽

Lord Jesus, I am often worried about many things—please grant me a heart like Mary, who rested at Your feet.

VERSE INDEX